ME

life is poetry

SÁLID SIMS

Table Of Content

Red Light 2
Hold Me 4
Stand Up 6
Desire 8
Pressure 10
It's True 12
Overdue Conversation 14
Protect Me 16
My First Time 18
Braided 20
Radiate You 22
Anniversary Flower 24
You 26
Heavens Cloud 28
The Perfect Sit Down 30
A Wife's Whisper 32
I've Walked Alone 34
Stratford Rd 36
Scarz 38
4 Play 40
Wherever You Go 42
War Of The Mirror 44
21-25 46
Benchmark Therapy 48
Rehabilitation 50
Worry Not 53
Meet The Author 54

ME: *life is poetry*

"We delight in the beauty of the butterfly,
but rarely admit the changes it has gone through
to achieve that beauty."

— *Maya Angelou*

Red Light

Time has told us that we're tired.
Tired of the screams...tired of the yells.
Time has told us that we can't wait;
Can't wait for safety...can't wait for understanding.
Time has become a napkin for us;
To wipe away the tears...to soak up the blood.
How can we look around and see rainbows when the clouds are so dark?
We continue to get instructions that are carried on the tail of every breeze,
not knowing that we can look within & find our freedom.

"If you want to fly, you have to give up the things that weigh you down."

— *Toni Morrison*

Hold Me

Hold me...hold me like I need you.
Hold me like letting me go is a crime.
Hold me like I shared space with you since you were in your mother's womb.
Hold me like I'm the creator of your world.
Hold me like our heartbeat is one.
Hold me like you want danger to be foreign to me.
Hold me like my life is a special gift to you...hold me and continue to teach me.
Hold me like years will become seconds.
Hold me like the right now is forever.
Hold me like our dreams connect with our reality.
To hold me is to hold yourself...So hold me.

"You have to decide who you are and force the world to deal with you, not with its idea of you."

— *James Baldwin*

Stand Up

I will not watch my brother struggle. My fist will not touch your face because you chose to step on my shoes.

I cannot continue to watch my sistas cry because I sold them a lie. My ignorance should not determine who you are as a Woman.

I will no longer hide behind a wall that I call my truth.
I'm afraid...afraid of being more than what I see.

Afraid of proving you wrong because that comes with responsibility.

I will not take the time to speak to my children w/o giving them life jewels. No longer will we set them up for failure from the lack of a proper example. This is harder than they will admit, but not as hard as we make it.

Keep some energy from our ancestors and add a bit of new age to it. I will not complain, and I will not put my foot to the pavement in an effort to change my reality.

A Queen is a Queen even if her ass is bouncing...I will not tear her down because I don't understand her struggle.

We can't continue to not be a safe place
Can't continue to think that they only need a dollar & a penis.

Stand up! It's time to STAND UP! We have to STAND UP!

"Hold fast to dreams, for if dreams die, life is a broken-winged bird that cannot fly."

— *Langston Hughes*

Desire

I desire to make you feel like a miracle.
To take away any fears that you may have.
You should feel the need to let your soul breathe around me.
Let your fingers touch my spirit and your lips sing songs to my heart.
I desire to be your comfort...to give your cravings rest.
Life has not been kind, but we will change that.
We will create a new world in 6 days and kiss passionately on the 7th.
The Sun will be our guide because I desire to show you things not often seen.
I need you to know how special you are.
Know that my sky is a blanket for you.
The ocean holds the waters that I will use to wash away your pain.
I know I haven't always shown you the utmost respect...but I desire to kiss your collarbone until sadness is a distant memory.
I desire to explore every part of you.
I want to feel every piece of what God created when you were in His mind.
I want your laugh to become a song to the world, and your passionate screams to be a symphony to my ears.
I desire to consume you...is that okay?

"The most common way people give up their power is by thinking they don't have any."

— *Alice Walker*

Pressure

Stop! It's way too hard and you don't have the resources.
Slow down! Don't give it your all because what if you fail?
Go! The time is now...only YOU can keep you from it.
Stop!

ME: *life is poetry*

"All that you touch, you change.
All that you change, changes you."

— *Octavia Butler*

It's True

Unconditional love is a crazy concept because you have to be crazy to give it. It means that you love someone regardless of how they treat you or make you feel.

A lot of times we give it to those who benefit from it a lot more than we do.

We give that gift to our children, but is it at all possible to give it to a spouse?

If your son steals from you, will you detach yourself from him?

If your daughter betrays you...could you never speak to her again?

What if you find that your husband has been sexting someone else?

We have to connect on much more than a physical level if we want to taste even 1% of unconditional love in a relationship.

"The present moment is filled with joy and happiness. If you are attentive, you will see it."

— *Thich Nhat Hanh*

Overdue Conversation

Nah...I'm not upset at all.
I had dinner with that woman and then slept outside for 3 nights.
Nah...I'm not upset at all.
I finally get in only to be told that you don't want me anymore.
Noooo...I'm not upset at all.
You had every right to call the police and put my life in danger.
Have them come inside our home & risk our children seeing their father in cuffs or a black bag.
Nah...I'm not upset at all.
I left when I should've stayed through it all and tried to work it out.
I should've listened to you more and tapped into what you needed from me.
Maybe I wasn't mature enough to be married in the first place.
Nah...I'm not upset at all.
I just continue to make excuses...continue to try to hold you when there's nothing to hold.
No...I'm not upset at all.
People change, and lives change...but the hurt remains the same.
I'm sorry that we were upset at all.

"Real ones appreciate real things."

— *Salid*

Protect Me

I stumbled across the floor learning to walk.
Life was so new to me and unexpected.
I've looked at the sky thinking that I could touch a cloud.
I didn't know who you left me with, but I know that you had to.
You had to work in order for me to eat
You couldn't have known that he would touch me.
I know that you didn't know that they beat me for no reason.
He would make me stay behind so that no one would see him kiss me.
I was so scared to stay there, but what could I have said?
What could I do when they ate our good food and gave us slop?
I used to wonder what would happen when I got older...
What would I do when I see you and I have some size?
Would I keep going or would I punish you for everything that you did to me?
Would I destroy your new life and cause your family to feel the pain that I felt?
I wanted to scream out for my Father but would he have heard me? Would you have hit me if I told?
The fear that is put into the victim is crippling...
Your body stops, and it seems like time doesn't exist.
You look into the future self as if it is right in front of you.
I hate this!
I hate that it has to be this way.
I hate that we live in a world that has so many demons in it that we don't know what an angel looks like anymore.
We can't be perfect.
We won't get it all right.
We will miss some things that are right in front of us.
Just help me... Protect me.

"When you do things from your soul, you feel a river moving in you, a joy."

— *Rumi*

My First Time

"Come and Talk To Me"...that played over and over in my mind.
The grass smelled like ginger for some reason
Every time I looked at you it felt like the first time.
I'm guessing that you knew how nervous I was because you giggled whenever you would look at me too.
Our conversation was easy flowing but it didn't seem to have much substance.
Two young people with urges that adults are supposed to act on.
Should I make a move to see how you will respond?
Do I tell you that you're beautiful and go in for a kiss?
So many things were going through my mind.
You grabbed my hand and told me to sit with you.
Sit with you even though there was only your seat to be in.
I think I understand...you want me to place you on my lap and we both occupy one space.
You want me to focus on your lips and have a taste.
I'm holding and caressing you like I know what I'm doing.
The entire time I'm playing back images that I've seen on TV or heard in my favorite R&B songs.
While I'm kissing you and you're touching me I start to wonder if it's really going to happen.
Am I going to cross the line from being a boy to becoming a Man?
You asked if I want to make love and though I don't rightfully know what making love is, I calmly tell you "Yes" as we continue to kiss.
I stand up and you lay back on your rainbow lawnchair as you remove your underwear.
I expose myself and you guide me into your awaiting pleasure.
I quickly learned how to do what I hadn't done before.
I quickly learned that my emotions had more control over me than I thought they did.
I learned so much My First Time.

"The soul becomes dyed with the color of its thoughts."

— *Marcus Aurelius*

Braided

She looked at me and poured into me like I was a cup, and she was water from the highest mountain.
My moments are paused by her presence, and sight is cleared by her light.
There's nothing that would keep me from creating more happiness with her.
The afterlife will be blessed with the interlocking of our hands.
Our children will feed off the vibrations from our heartbeat...can you feel it?
There's something liberating about opening our minds to truth.
The truth of knowing that though our time is short..our memories will sleep in infinity.
There's no force greater than the force that is US.

Stay with me...

"If you are always trying to be someone else, who will be you?"

— *Zora Neal Hurston*

Radiate You

Take the time to relax in a sunray.
Ride the energy until it carries you to the peace within the clouds.
The mountains will continue to look up to you for wisdom..while the valley will embrace the touch of your footsteps.
Power is a close friend of yours and virtue is your soulmate.
Grace will overwhelmingly consume you while also guiding you to heaven's gate.
Can a star even hope to shine brighter than thee?
Bright as your spirit.. which is overwhelming.
Breathe in all that you have created and hold all that you're still molding.

"Life without love is like a tree without blossoms or fruit."

— *Khalil Gibran*

Anniversary Flower

I saw you before I knew you.
I felt you before we ever touched.
Your words caressed my ears and danced on my soul.
Your voice plays the most beautiful music.
I often think about what life would be like without you.
It's in that moment that I wipe tears from my eyes.
Our connection could never be stronger, but I'm willing to give it a try.

"Love recognizes no barriers. It jumps hurdles, leaps fences, penetrates walls to arrive at its destination full of hope."

— *Maya Angelou*

YOU

YOU are magnificent.
YOU are in control.
YOU are love.
YOU are more precious than gold.
YOU are joy.
YOU are happiness.
YOU are resilient.
YOU erase sadness.
YOU are nurturing
YOU are mesmerizing.
YOU are fierce.
YOU are Queen.

"Each contact with a human being is so rare, so precious, one should preserve it."

— Anaïs Nin

Heavens Cloud

Your lips were moving, but your eyes said hello.
You spoke to me in a tone that I wasn't used to and that caused me to be intrigued.
I thought that I had this thing figured out but inadvertently you have me at a standstill.
My skin is tingling, and I don't even know your handle.
Her, She, Queen, or Goddess isn't important right now...
Right now, I'm in a trance from the visual that makes you... YOU.
In a trance due to the magnetic personality that you're allowing me to see.

ME: *life is poetry*

"What lies behind us and what lies before us are tiny matters compared to what lies within us."

— *Ralph Waldo Emerson*

The Perfect Sit Down

I've walked this road more times than I would like to remember
Did you give me this journey because I'm strong enough for it or do you have a sick sense of humor?
I realize that we can't all be the same, but why do some seem to have it so easy?
Why can some do what they want with little consequence, and I'm punished for the slightest slip-up?

"One who gains strength by overcoming obstacles possesses the only strength which can overcome adversity."

— Albert Schweitze

A Wife's Whisper

I knew that you were mine when our eyes connected.
Our story began before we even knew that our souls would merge.
You've protected me even when I didn't think I needed protection.
My love for you doesn't end because we can embrace no more.
The strength that you've shown me must now be used for our babies.
Those beautiful gifts that I was blessed to share with you.
I've never known a love like the one that you showed me.
Never known a touch as gentle as yours.
Our journey was filled with laughs, hugs, and sweet kisses.
Even when the storms came, we sought shelter in one another's smile.
I will forever be grateful for the time that I spent with you.
Know that you have made my existence worthwhile.

"The mirror will only lie to you if you've been lying to yourself."

— *Brandi Snyder*

I'VE WALKED ALONE

I don't want your help.
I've watched how you help people.
I never saw my Father kneel to anyone.
His pain was silent and escaped my sight.
I figured that my hands should create everything that I would ever need.
My eyes should see everything that I would need to see.
How was I able to enter certain rooms with no one showing me the door?
Is it a flex to aspire to not need an extended hand even when I'm on the ground floor?
Anxiety keeps me with strong toes and a mobile neck.
My level of trust is so low that it's nonexistent.
Raindrops land on me slowly if at all.
The wind walks with me and talks to me as the trees listen.
Do not pity the bird that flies alone;
Pity the chicken that has to share the coop.

"Although the world is full of suffering, it is also full of the overcoming of it."

— *Helen Keller*

Stratford Rd

I wrote this in my phone.
I wrote this in my phone because I didn't want you to miss what's in my brain.
When I write on paper other things fight to stain.
Stain the words that are food for a wanting brain.
Stain the words that are good for someone's gain.
I apologize in advance because this time I won't scream.
This time my voice will be as calming as the sea that they tricked my forefathers into sailing.
Calm until those glorious bodies entered those waters.
Don't tell me to stop now when I'm thinking about the pain of those sons, mothers, fathers, and daughters.
Those aunties, uncles, and cousins;
Nah...I won't raise my voice for this one.
I need you to be entranced by the sounds that my lips make on this one.
Blinding me with the cost of gas and food..hoping that I wouldn't concentrate on this one.
You have to wake up damn early to pull one on this One.
I can call myself a God if I feel or know that I am his Son.
Can I not?
Is it your place to stop me from believing what my soul has told me from day one?
Is your life journey to try to stop mine from crossing happiness's red ribbon?
I think not. See I'm in control of what makes my heart skip a beat.
I'm now in control of how smooth the asphalt is up under my feet.
This didn't just start today. It didn't start with me overly thinking about said circumstances.
This started on Stratford Rd.

"Out of suffering have emerged the strongest souls; the most massive characters are seared with scars."

— *Kahlil Gibran*

SCARZ

I see you in that picture trying to cover up what you see as a flaw..don't do that.
I understand that it may be because some Man didn't notice what I see and just wanted to hit that.
Your walk is your frame, and you don't have to explain that.
Just try your very best to love you and accept that.
I've gazed inside your chest plate and believe me, it's beautiful.
There should be no shame because you've had to do things that some may call despicable.
I don't claim to understand the thought process that caused some of your decisions.
But I do know that circumstances can sometimes sway us to do whatever to make provisions.
That phone screen is telling you that you have to look like every Woman sitting beachside.
While leaving out the truth embraces the beauty that's on the inside...
The size of your body should never outweigh the size of your character.
The integrity of your existence shouldn't change because the world tries to battle ya.
You smile while carrying the load of your world and it's so inspiring.
As a Man, I also understand that those forced smiles can sometimes get tiring.
Don't ever feel like you can't or shouldn't express those pains that continue to shape you.
While doing so make sure that healing light doesn't escape you.

"Deal with yourself as an individual, worthy of respect and make everyone else deal with you the same way."

— *Nikki Giovanni*

4 Play

Then I'm going to let my hands explore your body while we engage in a heart-stopping kiss.

Letting your river prepare to flow while my hands meet your breast, and my mouth is introduced after.

Open up your legs so that you're good and ready when I decide to part that sweet spot that I call "Her Heaven" ...

"Connection is the energy that exists between people when they feel seen, heard, and valued."

— *Brené Brown*

Wherever You Go

You don't have to change the way you look, but if you do, I'm in support of you.
In support of your grind, your time, and the glory of your intangibles.
Your strength has opened my eyes to new understandings of love.
Your touch has caused me to float beyond the ideas that rest above us.
Take whatever turn you like and whatever step you feel will progress you.
Know that you will never fall with me.
Know that I will be your biggest supporter and your protection when the ravens fly at night.
Your heart will be my resting place, and my peace will swim in your soul.
Don't feel like you can't be yourself with me.
Never feel like the true you will not be seen by me.
There is never a moment when you aren't with me... even when I can't be seen.
I've given too much of myself to a cold world to now let you slip away.
Know that you are all powerful and your intelligence is beyond the understanding of most.
Know that I will go wherever you go.

"The man who views the world at 50 the same as he did at 20 has wasted 30 years of his life."

— *Muhammad Ali*

War Of The Mirror

It feels good.
I look at myself and genuinely feel good.
Knowing what I know about what I did and what I am somehow still leaves me with the thought of being great.
No matter the tears that I produce or the frowns that I create I still end up with a smile.
There is nothing that can be said to me that will make me examine myself.
There isn't a person who could make me go right when my flesh wants to go left.
What am I doing here?
Is it normal to be wrong and feel absolutely nothing?
To destroy hearts and continue to collect them like golden coins.
There's something wrong with this picture
I know this with everything in me, but I continue to love me.
I continue to walk in a direction that may not be best for me.
Who can stop me though? Who will be the hero? Who will save the world from a Man like me?

"Your destiny is never tied to anyone who left."

— T.D. Jakes

21-25

Push me…I need you to push me, baby.
Push me to be whatever it is that you need me to be.
Push me to be the smile that you longed to see from your father.
Push me to be the hugs that you wanted to get from your mother.
Can you push me, baby?
Push me to be the tingle that your friends told you their baby daddy was for them.
Push me to be those stacks that flow so freely from a Beverly Hills ATM.
Push me to be that voice that stands up for us when the hope seems grim.
Push me baby so that I don't walk out whenever you need me to help you raise them.
Push me to be the loyal body that doesn't share his body just because another body is calling out to him.
Push me so that I see the beauty in you even though you may not be accustomed to feeling or seeing it yourself.
Push me so that I will open your door whether you need me to or not.
Push me so that I will sit facing the door, just in case someone comes to try and disrupt the spot.
Can you push me, baby?
Can you push me so that my lies taste like poison and the truth is the only cure?
Will you push me to communicate and work it out even when my flesh isn't sure?
I need you to push me, baby!
Push me so that I won't make the same mistakes that some made before me.
Push me so that when I'm gone it can truly be on a trip to glory.
Push me so that I can finally see what I need to see.
Push me so that I realize that the most important push will come from me.

ME: *life is poetry*

"There are years that ask questions and years that answer."

— *Zora Neale Hurston*

Benchmark Therapy

I took down a star today.
I put it in my pocket because I didn't want anyone else to see it.
I ran to the quietest spot I could find because I was overjoyed and thought that I might scream from excitement.
I found myself in the middle of the forest before I felt safe enough to examine my prize.
To hold it was like holding the warmest piece of peace to ever exist.
To listen to it was like hearing my Mother's whisper in the morning time.
To study it was like getting wisdom from my Father's hidden thoughts.
It makes me smile to think about being in my star's presence forever and saddens me to know that forever isn't possible.
What will I do?

"If I didn't define myself for myself, I would be crunched into other people's fantasies for me and eaten alive."

— *Audre Lorde*

Rehabilitation

You see...this is when it all started for me.
I was about 3, my Dad would put me on his knee, and smile at me so lovingly.
Who am I fooling? That may be someone's story, but it's not my reality.
The real journey as I recall...started at about 5.
My parents gave us love through actions, and I'm sure it was a task just to stay alive.
Now this consisted of both parents working while giving us all of the attention to seem like we were normal.
I know that they couldn't know that some of their choices would bring us such turmoil.
I remember having to stay with church members while they worked the night shift.
Their oldest boy was always offering things, but I knew early on that it was no gift.
Time and time again they stole our food and dared us to cry.
Smiling in our parent's faces, but forcing me to enter his backside.
These are things that a young mind remembers.
Back then there was no safety on the other side of the phone.
This was only the tip of the iceberg...y'all sit back as I go on.
When I was 7, while looking for the change from my milk money, I missed the bus.
So, I chose to go home with another church member... let's see if I have better luck.
This was a 17-year-old girl, and by today's standards would be called "thick".
She told me to go outside so she could play with my pixie stick.
The things she taught me that day were sickening and confusing.
The chain reaction caused more hurt because now it was my classmates, and I was doing the abusing.
A lost 9-year-old boy with all of this love around him.
My parents were married, Aunts, Uncles, and older cousins were all in love,

and I always wanted that to be me.
What was love though? Was it all about the physical, and did it look like these things that had happened to me?
Or was it more of a spiritual thing?
Like some of the Bible stories that were told to me?
These are some of the things that shaped me and turned me into the beast that you see.
I always wanted to do the right thing, but I'm not sure if that life was destined for me.
All of the hard and thoughtless times seemed to only make me angry.
Then I got good at hiding that emotion and only showing what I wanted people to see.
They say, "Hurt people hurt people", and if that's true then I must be broken.
I've hurt enough people to fill up the sea, and I fear that I'm just getting started.
How can you know that you're blessed but feel cursed at the same time?
It's like every time I advance...a part of me wants to hit rewind.
Gather around this worldly table and embrace me if you please.
There's so much more that I have to release before there will be rehabilitation for me.

"I have discovered in life that there are ways of getting almost anywhere you want to go, if you really want to go."

— *Langston Hughes*

WORRY NOT

Your prayers are laid upon the table of the Most High. Everything that should be... will be.

MEET THE AUTHOR

SÁLID SIMS

Salid Sims grew up as the second child of four in Greenville, SC, in a Christian/Bible-based home. From an early age, he focused on caring for his mother, siblings, and himself. After receiving his GED at age 27, Salid earned an associate degree in business management and certification in Robotics. He is now an entrepreneur and the founder of the podcast Kingshid Talk on his YouTube channel, Kingshid Productions. Salid is an avid chess player, enjoys reading, and especially loves watching movies with loved ones. He is a very observant person who is always optimistic and encouraging, believing that success requires determination, drive, strategy, and self-love.

At On the Write Track, we are committed to being a dynamic, faith-based, one-stop literary agent and consulting firm for aspiring authors who desire to self-publish and flourish in the marketplace. Our mission is to empower you, the author, by handling the details—such as book cover design,  website creation, editing, events, and more—so you can focus solely on what matters most: your message. We are here to guide you every step of the way, ensuring your literary journey is smooth and successful. Please contact us at publishuoo@gmail.com for more information.

www.ingramcontent.com/pod-product-compliance
Lightning Source LLC
LaVergne TN
LVHW010618070526
838199LV00063BA/5191